Focus on

Wuthering Heights

by Emily Brontë

Matt Simpson

GREENWICH EXCHANGE
LONDON

Greenwich Exchange, London

Focus on
Wuthering Heights

First published in Great Britain in 2007

Printed and bound by Q3 Digital/Litho, Loughborough
Tel: 01509 213456
Typesetting and layout by Albion Associates, London
Tel: 020 8852 4646
Cover design by December Publications, Belfast
Tel: 028 90286559

Greenwich Exchange Website: www.greenex.co.uk

Cataloguing in Publication Data is available from the British Library

ISBN-13: 978-1-906075-10-1
ISBN-10: 1-906075-10-7

for my daughter Catherine – to remind her
from where she got her name

Acknowledgements

I wish to thank John Farrell and Angela Topping for sharing their enthusiasms with me, and especially Professor John Lucas for his painstaking reading and for here and there justly putting me right.

O! dreadful is the check – intense the agony –
When the ear begins to hear, and the eyes begin to see;
When the pulse begins to throb – the brain to think again –
The soul to feel the flesh, and the flesh to feel the chain.

Emily Brontë

But she is in her grave, and oh,
The difference to me!

Wordsworth

Contents

Introduction

It now seems strange to us, with nearly a hundred years of 'experimental' writing behind us, that Emily Brontë's awe-inspiring novel should have received such bad notices on publication. Victorian sensibilities were not prepared to entertain anything like it. For one thing most novel readers of the time knew very little about Yorkshire and certainly not its remoter parts.[1] One of the most complexly structured work of fiction in the language (Walter Allen has described it as "perfect" and "the most remarkable novel in English"[2]) was deemed "coarse and loathsome", "utterly hateful", "wildly grotesque"; its plot was considered "sprawling". To what degree Emily Brontë knew she was breaking new ground is impossible to say. Or whether the novel was meticulously pre-planned or grew organically. It remains, however, a unique and highly original work and, properly read, the reading experience is compulsive. Once Emily Brontë has grabbed your attention – and she does this very swiftly – there's no way of escape.

And yet there are some people who find it difficult to get into easily. This is because they assume that the pompous style of its first narrator, which they see as off-putting, is going to be the style of the rest of the book and therefore fail to see that Emily Brontë is mercilessly sending Lockwood up.

I have a fancy that, when the Brontë sisters were discussing their idea of writing novels, the idea of bringing an effete gentrified southerner (like Mr Collins, say, from Jane Austen's *Pride and Prejudice*[3]) up north (something Mrs Gaskell is to echo in *North and South* published in 1854–5) and exposing him to life-in-the-raw on the Yorkshire moors, was something pleasurably talked over. If so, it was a brilliant one: it gave Emily the opportunity not only to create a comically satirical portrait of a silly, 'posh' southern townie but also provide herself with a narrator whose crass misjudgements oblige readers to read between the lines and become more profoundly involved in the story than he could ever be. It requires us to contemplate deeper matters than he is capable of comprehending. It is the reader who is made more desperately hungry than Lockwood for the 'explanation' Nelly Dean provides from chapter 4 onwards. He, in the role of listener, is no more than mildly curious, merely wanting to be 'entertained' while bored in bed recovering from a chill. The first three chapters scare us more than they scare him and it is part of the novel's brilliant technique to detach us from him after three chapters and hand us over to the ostensibly more common-sensible Nelly.

So, once read, what kind of novel do we say it is? Since publication it has been endlessly pored over and analysed, resulting in a plethora of interpretations.

For one thing it is a historical novel. It begins in 1801, seventeen years before Emily was born, and takes us back some thirty years before that. The dates 1771 (where Nelly starts her narrative) and 1801 offer a contrast of two centuries. The latter puts us firmly in a new century and may well indicate – the French Revolution taking place in 1789 and the American Declaration of Independence in 1776 – that we have been through revolutionary times. The turbulent passions of the book, the rebellious nature of some of its characters, its opposing Nature and Reason, passion and civilised values (seen as a veneer) are all important, as is the suggestion that out of this monstrous struggle a new dawn is possible – in the novel's case, the love between the second Catherine and Hareton. This is not to say it is a political novel but simply to suggest it has things in common with the spirit of the times in which it was written. Nor would it be right to think of it exclusively as a novel of racism – Heathcliff's dark-skinned hue has tempted some commentators to take it as such[4] – or of class, one in which one of the lowest-of-the-low, like an untouchable in India, rises up the social scale to become a gentleman and property-owner by doing down his social superiors. These elements are, without doubt, present, but to isolate them as paramount is to rob the novel of its complexity.

Most people read it as a love story, one that finds parallels in the kind of adolescent yearning – which many harbour at a deep level of their psyches – for an absolute can't-live-without attachment, a total identification with a soul-mate – that is if we see the novel as primarily 'about' the passionate yet curiously asexual relationship of Heathcliff and Catherine Earnshaw, a relationship which can only find fulfilment in death. But there are several kinds of love in the book (all of them painful in one way or another): filial love (children for parents, parents for children); the kind that may or may not exist in the marriages between Catherine and Edgar, Hindley and Frances, Heathcliff and Isabella – each of which is procreative and destructive at the same time. Then, at a less exalted level, there is the "over head and ears" feeling Lockwood experienced which made him run away from the girl at the seaside who simply looked "the sweetest of all imaginable looks" at him and therefore obliged him to seek out a "misanthropist's heaven"; and then there is his fancying the second Catherine, a feeling that is still present when he returns in 1802. Finally we have the hopefully redemptive love-relationship between the second Catherine and Hareton, whose marriage takes place (outside the novel) in 1803. So if we say it is a novel about love, there are all these aspects of it to consider, and much of its 'meaning' comes from the contrasts these all make available.

It is certainly a work in which extraordinary emotions are registered, in which violent passion (tenderness in it is exceptional) is consistently and directly associated with natural forces (rain, storm, aggressive dogs) and over-shadowed by illness and death. Hardly a character escapes illness of one form or another; there are eleven deaths. It deals in the basic facts of life: birth (explicitly connected with death), unglamourised childhoods and adolescence, unsentimentalised love and its connected opposite, hate, as well as cruelty, vengeance, greed, separation and unwelcome intrusions into the lives of others. We may be tempted into thinking the events of the novel occur in a fierce amoral universe in which struggle for survival in life and beyond death is paramount. What we are being asked to do is make a leap into the grave and whatever lies beyond it – a grave that mummifies its occupants in peat-mould and releases their souls not into Christian heaven but out into the rugged landscape of the moors.

We could read it as a *Bildungsroman*, concerned with following the progress from childhood to adulthood – though, one has to say, it is hardly a textbook on how to bring up children! Children are either abused and/or spoilt; and they all have a propensity for violence. Weakness throughout the novel is despised.[5] Nelly is perhaps the only really grown-up person in it who, having attained the age of 44 when the novel starts, is to a degree able to reflect on her experiences and interpret them with a modicum of common sense. The other characters are, in varying degrees, stunted like the firs at Wuthering Heights. If we think of the novel as a *Bildungsroman* it is most likely we will focus less on the rites of passage of what we might call the first generation – Heathcliff, Hindley, Catherine, Edgar – than on the genesis and growing-up of the second Catherine and Hareton. If we think this way, it is what we will judge the novel to be ultimately 'about'.

Some see it as a Gothic tale about a 'demon lover' and indeed there are traces of Gothic melodrama in it: the grinding teeth, the hanging of dogs, the ghostly wrist rubbed against the broken glass, the ancient carving over the door of Wuthering Heights, leaping into graves, emotional excesses. But *Vathek* or *The Castle of Otranto* it is not. Emily Brontë is not dealing in stereotypical characters and situations; she is not offering simple titillations but something intensely more realistic and profound. It may be more pertinent to point out that Emily Brontë, like many others at that time, almost certainly read Goethe's *Werther* in which the hero, an artist with a melancholy sensibility, at odds with society, falls desperately in love with a girl engaged to someone else and ends up committing suicide.

In that its setting is the Yorkshire moors, one may legitimately describe it as a regional novel, one, like others soon to emerge (like *Mary Barton*) that sets out to introduce readers to new and unfamiliar territory (see note 1). Its use of dialect, for one thing, sets it apart.[6] Or then again it is possible to see it as a poetic novel – poetic in the sense that it shares the passionate spirit, the response to landscape, the imaginative intensity, the energy we find in the Romantic poets. Indeed some critics associate Heathcliff with the Byronic hero and some find echoes of Walter Scott in the book and read it as a novel of romantic heroism. But, as I hope to show, it is not a dramatic poem but a novel that shows a profound understanding and implementation of the resources of prose narrative.

There is no doubting it is a great and powerful ghost story, one in which a ghost attempts to get in and a haunted man yearns to get out. The ghost of Catherine Earnshaw/ Linton (like the marriage of her daughter to Hareton) exists 'outside' the novel, a ghost trying and eventually succeeding to get in it in order to release Heathcliff, a man "beguiled with the spectre of a hope through eighteen years",[7] from it. The book demands belief in an after-life existence very different from that believed in by Christians. (One can easily argue that *Wuthering Heights* is a deeply, if highly unorthodox, religious novel ... or, if you were a Joseph, an irreligious one).[8] The importance of contrast between 'outside' and 'inside' (as with soul and body)[9] is highlighted throughout by the constant reference to windows[10] and, to a lesser extent, doors, along with another very powerful motif that runs consistently through the work, that of characters acting as intruders or interlopers, including ourselves, the readers, voyeuristically intruding into emotional territory belonging to others. Most of the events in the novel are determined by people being where they shouldn't be.

Wuthering Heights is a story of painful separations as well as a simmering stew-pot of claustrophobic and disturbing relationships. Lockwood pathetically uses irony, euphemism and insouciance to protect himself from feelings, and Nelly Dean has her brand of shrewd commonsense. The reader is the one nakedly exposed.

Notes

[1] "That the Yorkshire of *Wuthering Heights* was an unknown country to novel readers is clear ... from the painstaking description of place in early chapters of Mrs Gaskell's *Life of Charlotte Brontë*, and from Charlotte's preface to the second edition of Emily's novel in 1850." Kathleen Tillotson, *Novels of the Eighteen-Forties* (Oxford University Press, 1961).

[2] Walter Allen, *The English Novel* (Penguin, 1970).

[3] Emily's sister Charlotte's views on Jane Austen are well known: "She ruffles her reader by nothing vehement, disturbs him by nothing profound. The passions are perfectly unknown to her: she rejects even a speaking acquaintance with that stormy sisterhood." Letter to W.S. Williams, 12th April 1850.

[4] I am indebted to John Lucas for the following observations: "Heathcliff's darkness. Fear of exogamy and of miscegenation run through the 19th century. Whether Heathcliff is a gypsy or octoroon or whatever, is less important than fear of him as possibly these things. The dark is exotic. It is also (therefore?) associated with unruly passion ... blonde women and men can be trusted, whereas dark-complexioned can't be. Emily Brontë is radical/ iconoclastic in implicitly challenging this."

[5] For instance, Heathcliff tells Nelly in chapter 21 he has taught Hareton "to scorn everything extra-animal as silly and weak". The sickly Linton Heathcliff is treated as a kind of degenerate. The chill-ridden Lockwood is a figure of fun.

[6] Though it is only fair to point out that Tennyson had already used dialect in poetry, and Scott in the novel; Elizabeth Gaskell on the other side of the Pennines is busy writing *Mary Barton* (published 1848), and eight years before *Wuthering Heights* Dickens had written *Nicholas Nickleby* with scenes set in Yorkshire.

[7] i.e. from the death of the first Catherine on 20th March 1784.

[8] Heathcliff declares: "No minister need come, nor need anything

be said over me." The kirk Lockwood notices at the end of the book is disused and in a state of decay. Joseph's religion is of the punitive hell-fire sort, more Old Testament than New, ruled over by Blake's God of the Thou-Shalt-Nots and Vengeance; it ironically injects a black demonic quality to the book. Only Nelly, we may feel, has the Blakean virtues of Mercy, Pity, Peace and Love that Christ, the God of the New Testament, represents.

9 A Jungian interpretation would involve the terms *animus* and *anima* and *integration*. In *An Introduction to Jung's Psychology* (Penguin, 1961) Frieda Fordham writes: "... the unconscious of a man contains a complementary feminine element, that of a woman a male element. These Jung calls respectively the *anima* and the *animus*."

10 Freud suggests that those who dream of windows, doors, keyholes, apertures of various kinds, are subconsciously encountering aspects of themselves they are refusing to confront consciously.

1

1801

It is on *re*-reading *Wuthering Heights* that one begins to realise how Emily Brontë makes her impact on the reader. She has invented cinematic techniques long before the cinema has come into being. Events are 'explained' in flashback and, for the most part, matter-of-factly (she keeps reminding us of the present by every so often tactfully returning to it). Yet at the same time there is this intense voyeuristic sense of up-close claustrophobic intimacy (intensified by bad weather), which she contrasts now and then with wide-panning shots of landscape.

The novel begins, extraordinarily, near the very end of its history. In fact it is staggering to realise, with the hindsight re-reading affords, that in 1801 certain highly significant events, yet to be disclosed, have only very recently taken place. Linton and the second Catherine were married in August; Edgar Linton has died in September and Linton Heathcliff in October – which means that Lockwood probably took over the tenancy of Thrushcross Grange very soon afterwards: chapter 30, in fact, makes it plain the twelve-month tenancy runs to the end of October 1802. Heathcliff therefore has wasted no time in securing the property for himself. When the novel opens, Heathcliff, though no one knows it yet, is on the brink of the longed-for reunion with the ghost of Catherine and has a mere six months of life left. We learn in the final chapter that he actually dies in the strange coffin-like bed Lockwood was traumatically forced to stay in just under a year before. Neither Lockwood nor the reader has any idea that 1801 has more to it than Lockwood's renting Thrushcross Grange and his bumbling visits to make himself known to his landlord. There are things that need 'explaining', things that puzzle and scare us in the first three chapters.

These three chapters pull Lockwood and the reader into an emotional maelstrom; Lockwood is both ignorant and oddly innocent: not only does he not know what he's letting himself in for, but he keeps making naïve misjudgements based on a sense of his own superiority. Ironically, the reader, able to see through him, is, in a sense, superior to him. In 1801 we can work out that, of the then-living whom Lockwood encounters (the dead are 'present' too – a woman dead seventeen years, who died at nineteen but who strangely 'returns' in the form of a twelve-year-old), Heathcliff is thirty-seven, Hareton twenty-three, the second Catherine seventeen, and Nelly forty-four; Lockwood is described as being a young man in chapter 25 and, as we know from chapter 1, is a stranger who has initially arrived in Yorkshire looking for a "misanthropist's heaven". He doesn't stay long: in chapter 30, judging that Nelly's story, though far from reaching a resolution, is over, he decides to go to London for six months; he then simply returns in the September of 1802 to "devastate the moors of a friend in the north". It is half-whim ("a sudden impulse seized me"), and partly the opportunity to settle financially with his landlord, that drives him to visit Thrushcross Grange and there hear the astounding pronouncement that Heathcliff has died three months previously in May. This news amazes him, but it doubly astonishes the reader by its blunt matter-of-factness. It is a brilliant piece of writing taking a major character out of the story "three months since". It ensures we still need Nelly if we are to keep hold on reason and common sense. In a novel teeming with the irrational, it is the reader's good sense which is at risk, much more than Lockwood's. For all the weird things that happen to him or what he is told, he walks out of the novel virtually unscathed.

Voyeurism is determined by the first thing on the first page: the date "1801". We are reading a journal[1]. This, written in the first person, should indicate a measure of authenticity in that it is almost certainly written up after the events it records. As when Lockwood reads Catherine's writings in bed at Wuthering Heights, there is the sense that we may be violating something intended as private or at least as personal. Is it vanity that compels Lockwood to record his comings and goings? Is he thinking of possible publication? Ironically this comes true by virtue of what we might call ghost-writing.

Whatever the case, it soon becomes apparent he has very little understanding of the events he is observing, taking part in and recording. He is the archetypical unreliable narrator.

Notes

[1] I am grateful to John Lucas for this gloss: *Wuthering Heights* "uses forms of narrative – especially journal – that are very much associated with a female view. (You could confide in a diary and/ or journal what you couldn't tell anyone else, and it allowed for speculation in a manner not permitted in 'discourse'. Male novelists get in on this act: *Bleak House* and, most tellingly perhaps, *The Woman in White*. But *Wuthering Heights* is the first great novel after Richardson to make significant use of this device)."

2

Where Time Stagnates

Until the end of chapter 30, the narration delivered to Lockwood, though swinging back some 30 years and then subsequently moving forward in leaps, 'happens' in 1801. Our first connection with the past, however, is through the date 1500 and the name "Hareton Earnshaw" carved over the main door of Wuthering Heights: this tells us that an Earnshaw family has lived there for at least 300 years and that it is no raggle-taggle farm but a building of some substance as well as a long history. Nelly Dean's narration, however, takes us back to 1771 when old Earnshaw walks to Liverpool, then moves forward to his death in 1777, then to Hareton's birth in 1778, Edgar Linton's proposal in 1780, his marriage to Catherine Earnshaw in 1783, Isabella's marriage to Heathcliff the following year 1784 – which year also contains the birth of Catherine Linton, the consequent death of her mother, and the death of the drunken Hindley, then through 1776 and 1797 to 1800 when Edgar catches a terminal chill, and finally back to 1801.

1801 is, until we reach chapter 32, our anchor in the narrated present. We are, remember, reading what Lockwood has written in his journal. But the journal is the container for more narratives than Lockwood's or Nelly's – there are reports of events within their narratives. For example, Catherine Earnshaw's diaries that Lockwood reads in chapter 3, in which she may be said to come alive; and within Nelly's version of events there are times she becomes the medium for other accounts of what has happened: for instance Isabella's letter in chapter 13, Zillah's account of Edgar's illness and death in chapter 30, Heathcliff explaining himself to Nelly in chapter 33. There are others too, as when a servant called Mary and a blacksmith's lass tell what they know; Joseph when he tells things to Nelly who then passes them on to Heathcliff in chapter 10; and even Doctor Kenneth add bits. Chapter 18 reports what villagers have to tell. Until we get to chapter 32, where suddenly we find we have moved on a year to 1802, the story takes perhaps a couple of days to tell (and however long it takes for us to read) while Lockwood lies in bed recovering. Until then we are constantly being reminded that 1801 is our present and that Nelly is addressing a Lockwood who is quite unaware that his journal is being read by anyone else – though his vanity might be stimulated by knowing it was. In chapter 7, for example, Lockwood begs Nelly, who wants at that point – but is not allowed – to skip three years to the death of Mr and Mrs Linton in 1780, to talk on for another half-hour; and in other places, for example at the end of chapter 9, Nelly chances "to glance towards the timepiece over the chimney" and breaks off her story to go to bed; in chapters 10 and 15, Lockwood himself briefly resumes the narrative. Nelly will, on occasion, directly address Lockwood, as when she says in chapter 25, "These things happened last winter, sir." At the end of chapter 14, Nelly's narration is interrupted by the arrival of Doctor Kenneth – this reminds us that Lockwood, lying in bed suffering from exposure, both physical and intellectual, is merely wishing to be entertained, indulging a simple curiosity spiced with naïve and perturbing romantic feelings he has for the second Catherine:

> Dree and dreary, I reflected, as the good woman descended to receive the doctor, and not exactly of the kind I should have chosen to amuse me. I'll extract wholesome medicines from Mrs Dean's bitter herbs; and firstly, let me beware the fascination that lurks in Catherine Heathcliff's brilliant eyes. I should be

> in a curious taking if I surrendered my heart to that young person, and the daughter turned out a second edition of the mother.

The next chapter begins with Lockwood announcing:

> Another week over, and I am so many days nearer health and spring! I have now heard all my neighbour's history, at different sittings, as the housekeeper could spare time from more important occupations. I'll continue it in her own words, only a little condensed. She is, on the whole, a very fair narrator, and I don't think I could improve her style.

A further instance happens in chapter 7 where Nelly says:

> But, Mr Lockwood, I forget these tales cannot divert you. I'm annoyed how I should dream of chattering on at such a rate, and your gruel cold, and you nodding for bed! I could have told Heathcliff's history – all that you need hear – in half a dozen words.

This is wit of a high order. The story could have perversely stopped just there. And the only reader response to this is: thank God it didn't! Emily Brontë does a very similar thing at the end of chapter 30 when Lockwood declares: "Thus ended Mrs Dean's story", and the only possible reader response is: not to my satisfaction it hasn't! Lockwood is about to go off to London for six months with no real intention of returning ("I wouldn't pass another winter here for much"), and so the author gives the impression of arbitrarily and alarmingly removing both of our main witnesses! Of course she brings Lockwood back the following year and, as we have already said, has him turn up some fourteen miles from Gimmerton to indulge in a bit of grouse-shooting. It's mere happenstance and "sudden impulse" that brings him back into the story, a story the reader psychologically is more in need of continuation than he. Luckily (it being September) there are still some weeks of tenancy left to him. And what does Emily Brontë do next but deliver the *coup de foudre* of Heathcliff's death three months earlier!

This constant and highly sophisticated manipulation of the reader's reactions through the creation of multiple perspectives is one of the novel's outstanding features. But it's more than this. The shifting about of the time sequence and the Chinese boxes containing the various narratives are part of a project to get somewhere beyond the normal and expected conditions of most people's lives. T.S. Eliot has a useful line in *Four Quartets*, which in a different way explores similar territory: he writes: "Only through time time is conquered." This is what Emily Brontë is primarily concerned with: adjusting the temporal world to something outside or beyond it. This is no ghost story written for the sake of titillating or vicariously scaring the reader – rather it is a project to 'prove' the existence of a supernatural dimension to human life or, if you like, the existence of the soul. Catherine Earnshaw asks Nelly: " ... surely you and everybody have a notion that there is or should be an existence of yours beyond you. What were the use of my creation if I were entirely contained here?" I say 'prove' because, given the intense imaginative involvement generated in us in our reading, the work does, in our inexorably highly-sensitised imaginations, give us no way out of believing in a condition – at least in the case of the first Catherine and Heathcliff – which transcends mundane existence. This is Coleridge's willing suspension of disbelief with a vengeance.

Emily Brontë delivers the *coup de grâce* at the end when she has Nelly report:

> ... an odd thing happened to me about a month ago. I was going to the Grange one evening – a dark evening, threatening thunder; and just at the turn of the Heights I encountered a little boy with a sheep and two lambs. He was crying terribly, and I supposed the lambs were skittish and would not be guided.
>
> "What's the, matter, my little man?" I asked.
>
> "There's Heathcliff and a woman yonder, under t'

> nab," he blubbered, "and I darnut pass 'em." I saw nothing; but neither the sheep nor he would go on ...

The psychological aptness is stunning. The lad knows Heathcliff well enough to name him but has no knowledge of the first Catherine, who died 18 years previously, hence the anonymous "woman". Nelly can offer excuses: the lad "probably raised the phantoms from thinking, as he traversed the moors alone, on the nonsense he had heard his parents and companions repeat". But she's not comfortable with this: the element of superstition in her make-up which she has confessed to several times obliges her to say: "Yet, I don't like being out in the dark now, and I don't like being left by myself in this grim house. I can't help it." What she doesn't acknowledge (but we are required to) is the fact that *the sheep* 'know' there's something there and "would not be guided". You can explain the little boy's anxieties away, but not those of the sheep. Which of course makes nonsense of Lockwood's God's-in-his-heaven judgement at the end, gazing at the three headstones, wondering how under a "benign sky ... any one could ever imagine unquiet slumbers for the sleepers in that quiet earth". Lockwood walks away from the graves and out of the novel; it is the reader who stands there a while longer, knowing that the experience he has lived through is not so easy to walk away from.

3

Terror Made Me Cruel

The first three chapters are crucial. They take us away from the familiar world we know into something remote; we leave, as Lockwood did, the "stir of society" behind us for something darkly primitive, vigorously anti-social, with undercurrents of ferocity capable of sudden eruption, a stormy world in which witchcraft, superstition and hell-fire religion seem a natural part of the fabric, where the people are inhospitable, wary of strangers, and wanting to be left to live out their bleak and gloomy – and private – lives. It is not the world of polite literature but one more akin to traditional ballad or folk-tale. We enter a place where people and dogs growl with suppressed or released anger, we then penetrate deeper (snowed in with no escape) into the even more enclosed, claustrophobic space of the coach- or coffin-like closet. At first we may, like Lockwood, sigh with some relief to be offered a modicum of protection. But the relief is short-lived, for from here we high-dive into a world beyond everyday consciousness, into violent dreams so vivid that the distinction between dream and reality is lost. In fact the ice-cold hand Lockwood rubs against the broken pane intrudes on reality (it is after all on the outside trying to get in, and blood, we are told, stains the bedclothes) to the point we feel it even exists outside and beyond as well as in the context of dream. This is very much part of the author's purpose described earlier of 'proving' existences beyond death; at the same time it obliges us to query what is *ever* actual. Consider how quickly this and our consequent willing suspensions of disbelief are determined and established in the novel. Dreams make havoc of Reason: Lockwood is reduced to a panic of madness and to the level of savagery he is pathetically trying to comprehend, and which he encounters in the brooding world of Wuthering Heights and its sullen master whose misanthropist's heaven he thinks he can share. It is a much *more real* misanthropist's heaven than Lockwood could ever have bargained for; more akin to limbo or what Coleridge calls "a nightmare life in death". It is, as we learn later, where Heathcliff "*lives*" ("O God! It is unutterable! I cannot live without my life. I cannot live without my soul!") in a condition of separation, brutally and malevolently detaining others with him; where spring can only return with his death, and restitution become possible through the second generation, with Cathy's sticking primroses in Hareton's porridge and the Earnshaw dynasty restored.

Our narrator has to be distrusted. He gives himself away by his language. Coming from the polite world, he uses language to impress – mainly himself. Offering his linguistic credentials to Heathcliff cuts no ice:

> 'Mr Lockwood, your new tenant, sir. I do myself the honour of calling as soon as possible after my arrival, to express the hope I that have not inconvenienced you by my perseverance in soliciting the occupation of Thrushcross Grange: I heard yesterday you had had some thoughts — '
>
> 'Thrushcross Grange is my own, sir,' he interrupted, wincing. 'I should not allow any one to inconvenience me, if I could hinder it – walk in!'

Chapter 1 sees Lockwood confronting things he has no emotional or intellectual equipment for dealing with, and so having slightly to modify his notions. Heathcliff is "a capital fellow" and "(he) and I are such a suitable pair to divide the desolation between us" are modified to "a man more exaggeratedly reserved than myself" and to "sullenly preceded me up the causeway", "surly", "rather morose". I say slightly because Lockwood learns very little from direct experience: in any case Heathcliff is soon put at a safe distance for him (is, as it were, fictionalised) by Nelly's narrative.[1]

We cannot escape judging him pompous in his speech and naïve in his actions and the conclusions he draws from them. We have already noted how he has run off up north because a young girl's glances in his direction panicked him. In this first chapter, for example, he is attacked by dogs (described as "four-footed fiends", "combatants", "possessed swine") and has to defend himself with a poker after stupidly provoking them "by winking and making faces at them". He is rescued by "a lusty dame" wielding a frying pan. Heathcliff, seeing him "flurried", offers him a glass of wine and they talk:

> I found him [Heathcliff] very intelligent on the topics we touched; and before I went home I was encouraged so far as to volunteer another visit tomorrow. He evidently wished no repetition of my intrusion. I shall go, notwithstanding. It is astonishing how sociable I feel myself, compared with him.

Of course we need him to go to Wuthering Heights again because our curiosities have been aroused as to who this strange "dark-skinned gypsy" called Heathcliff is, dressed like a gentleman; why he is morose, and who else – other than the "peevish" Joseph, who like an evil spirit, mumbles "indistinctly in the depths of the cellar" – may live there (Lockwood hears a "chatter of tongues and a clatter of utensils deep within"). Who is the "lusty dame" with the frying pan? We are now fully attuned to the irony that comes from the contrasts Emily Brontë clearly sets up as part of the substance of the narrative, particularly between what Lockwood perceives and what we more pertinently see. This irony is at one with the binary patterns that seem to shape the novel: the two houses, two brother/sister relationships, two Catherines, two sons (Hareton and Linton), the second

Catherine's two marriages, two principal narrators, and so on. And, momentously at this point in the novel, we have Lockwood's second trip to Wuthering Heights in which he will be attacked a second time by dogs and have two dreams.

But he nearly doesn't go ("I had half a mind to spend it [the day] by my study fire" ... even admitting this to be "a lazy intention"). What changes his mind is the sight of a maid "raising an infernal dust" at the study hearth. What this indicates – as we also see from other examples – is his continuing to alienate (and at the same time intrigue) us by being less interested in what he does than we are made to be. We retain too strong a hauntingly chiaroscuro impression of an ancient bleak house up on the stormy moors with its inhospitable inhabitants, its guns and dogs, its brooding atmosphere.

This time Lockwood travels the four miles on foot rather than taking his horse as he did in chapter 1. In this second chapter first impressions are confirmed and taken to a deeper level.

Incapable of reading the weather, he foolishly arrives as snow begins to fall (making the prospect of a four-mile walk back somewhat parlous) only to find the gate locked against him and nobody at home but Joseph and "'t' missis". It is at this point Emily Brontë introduces a gruff "young man without coat, and shouldering a pitchfork" who lets him into the house. There he tries to make conversation with the "missis", who, he falsely assumes, is "Mrs Heathcliff", and mistakes a heap of dead rabbits for pet cats. We notice how the house contains and feeds on the dead. Lockwood, though thinking her "unnatural", starts to cast a roving eye over the "missis". The young man hangs about the room, dismissed by Lockwood as "haughty". But here, did we but know it, we have a girl and a young man who will end up truly loving each other ("the one loving and desiring to esteem, and the other loving and desiring to be esteemed") and marrying in just over a year's time – symbolically on New Year's Day. Heathcliff makes a brusque appearance and rudely shouts at the missis, offending Lockwood's sense of gallantry to the point of his thinking: "The tone in which the words were said revealed a genuine bad nature. I no longer felt inclined to call Heathcliff a capital fellow." Thinking the missis is Heathcliff's wife, he earns himself the brutal sarcasm that Heathcliff's wife is dead and the rhetorical question: "Oh, you would intimate that her spirit has taken the post of ministering angel, and guards the fortunes of Wuthering Heights even when the body has gone. Is that it?" This, part of the psychological programming Emily Brontë is gradually bringing to bear on us, is to take on a shattering significance before the book ends. Lockwood now realising that Heathcliff must be forty (he is in fact thirty-seven) and that the missis "did not look seventeen" (for once right in his assumption) puts two and two together to make five, now reasoning that the "young man" (whom he snobbishly terms "clown") must be Heathcliff's son and "the favoured possessor of the beneficent fairy", i.e. the missis' husband. Lockwood can't get anything right and makes a fool of himself and feels, with only himself to blame, out of place and determined not to venture "under those rafters a third time".

But we now know that the missis is the wife of a son by Heathcliff and that the "clown" shares a name with the "Hareton Earnshaw" carved over the door. So there is more unravelling to do: where is the son, where is Heathcliff's wife, where does Hareton fit in, how come Heathcliff owns both Thrushcross Grange and Wuthering Heights, where does the beneficent fairy come from, why does the missis menace Joseph with witchcraft, why is everyone ill-tempered, and what is this we hear from Joseph about the missis having inherited the ill-nature of her mother, who, he is certain, went straight to the devil?

Lockwood wants to get back home but is trapped by the weather. No-one is willing to guide him, and now, against his will, he is "compelled to stay". But hearing the bad-tempered bickering going on between Hareton, Heathcliff and Mrs Heathcliff, he grabs a lantern and tries to make his own way, only to be attacked by two dogs whom he pretentiously berates with "several incoherent threats of retaliation, that, in their indefinite depth of virulency, smacked of King Lear", ending up with a nose-bleed. No wonder Heathcliff and Hareton guffaw. It is Zillah who comes to his rescue with a pint of ice water splashed down his neck. After a brandy, he is "compelled perforce to accept lodgings" under Heathcliff's roof. This second visit is much more unsettling: Lockwood's pretensions to civilised values are assaulted and his nerve-endings are starting to fray a little. Whatever his intentions, they are all now frustrated. But worse is to come.

Chapter 3 sees Zillah escorting Lockwood to his bedroom and mumbling about "queer goings-on" at some unspecified time. Clambering into the coach-like closet/bed, he embarks upon a journey into a deeper stage of consciousness, intruding into an even more private zone, that of someone's childhood, evidenced by names scratched on the paintwork, a diary and the marginal jottings in mildewed books. He is doing what the reader is doing. The names surprise us: *Catherine Earnshaw*, *Catherine Linton*, *Catherine Heathcliff*. Here in condensed form is the whole story. It is that last name which sets the pulse racing. As Lockwood slides into sleep (into that other kind of consciousness the novel insists on), the names become "vivid as spectres". A smell of burning leather startles him from reverie: it is tantamount to an act of sacrilege. As he reads the words of the diary, a relationship between the writer and Heathcliff and their love of the wild moors and rebellious natures (they fling their books into the dog kennel) emerge; the past becomes alive in the present. The pair suffer a three-hour-long sermon from Joseph and we learn of Heathcliff enduring harsh treatment at the hands of Hindley, a character new to us. Are there mitigating circumstances then to help us understand the surly Heathcliff, now somewhere in another part of the house?

Lockwood picks up a book by the Reverend Jabes Branderham, with its hypnotic or spell-like title, *Seventy Times Seven and the First of the Seventy-First*. It is this that sinks him into sleep and plunges him into a dream of "old transgressions that I never previously imagined", of Old Testament vengefulness that for all the world feels like an aspect of primitive tribal consciousness. The dream in which he is denounced before a congregation wanting to "Drag him down, and crush him to atoms" clearly symbolically re-enacts his experience earlier with the dogs. He wakes to find the branch of a fir tree has been tapping at the window. He dozes and enters another dream ... or state of consciousness that allows ghosts to appear: more vision than dream, more real than real. The ice-cold hand of a child (we should note here for later reference the fact that Catherine appears as a twelve-year-old and not the age, some seven years on, at which she died) is desperately trying to force entrance through the window into the room. Lockwood for all his breeding and good manners panics:

> Terror made me cruel; and finding it useless to attempt shaking the creature off, I pulled its wrist on the broken pane, and rubbed it to and fro till the blood ran down and soaked the bedclothes.

These images cut deeply and vividly into our consciousness and we are appalled by his brutality; and our perplexity and horror are further exploited by the scratching and pushing of the books Lockwood hastily piles against the hole in the windowpane. We have now forgotten this is a dream; it is more like the medium ghosts exist in: as with the little lad's sheep at the novel's end, we know something is *there* and there is no escaping a strange pang of pity that the ghost has been abused and savagely rejected. Again, this is willing suspension of disbelief with a vengeance.

In answer to his yelling, Heathcliff comes charging into the room and Lockwood witnesses, as he describes it, "a piece of superstition on the part of the landlord which belied oddly with his apparent sense" and he (tactlessly) shouts out something about "ghosts and goblins", calling the subject of his visitation "a changeling", "a minx", "a wicked little soul" justly punished "for her mortal transgressions, I've no doubt". Again, he has learnt nothing from the experience and simply goes into his usual self-protective mode; he acts, as ever, as someone offended rather than jolted by his experience. The reader is left with an ambivalent feeling of compassion. His landlord breaks into an uncontrollable passion of tears:

> Come in! ... Cathy, do come! Oh, do – *once* more! Oh, my heart's darling! Hear me *this* time, Catherine, at last!

It is important to register that the "once more" and "this time" mean that this ghost has manifested herself before.

Lockwood is embarrassed but, despite himself, experiences an odd pang of compassion for his landlord. But Heathcliff and Catherine are isolated in a region beyond his comprehension – in other words the imaginations of the readers.[2]

But it doesn't end there for Lockwood. Next morning he finds Heathcliff morosely abusing the second Catherine.

Glad to be back at the Grange, Lockwood's "human fixture" (Nelly!) and "her satellites" rush to greet him. The tension is slackened by a return to the unconsciously comic manner he has of describing things and to the 'normality' of warmth, concern and a smoking cup of coffee.

The first three chapters then prime us for the narrative that begins in chapter 4. They unhinge us from reliance on rational explanations for things. Lockwood, despite going through traumatic experiences and revealing cruel aspects of his nature, is, we soon discover, merely curious about the inhabitants of Wuthering Heights and their history. It is the reader who hurries, like a distressed patient to a therapist, to Nelly Dean for her hopefully sober account of things.

Notes

[1] " ... the patterns are all psychoanalytically recognisable, as though Emily Brontë had an exceptionally clear channel of

communication with the subconscious. The psychologically threatening material is encompassed and made just safe enough in a most carefully structured narrative form ..." David Skilton, *Defoe to the Victorians: Two Centuries of the English Novel* (Penguin, 1985).

[2] "Emily Brontë makes no distinction between the natural and the supernatural: her world is one and, rendered ever so concretely as it may be, it is a spiritual world." Walter Allen, *The English Novel.*

4

A Steady, Reasonable Kind of Body

We cannot trust Lockwood's account and yet in a sense it is all we have. Half-way through the novel, in chapter 15, we are told he'll continue Nelly's story "in her own words, only a little condensed", which reminds us he is writing up what he has been told and suggests that a degree of editing, however slight, is and has been going on. It raises the question of how accurate Nelly's story is. At the end of chapter 7 she is allowed to say:

> I certainly esteem myself a steady, reasonable kind of body ... not exactly from living among the hills and seeing one set of faces and one series of actions from year's end to year's end, but I have undergone sharp discipline, which has taught me wisdom; and then I have read more than you would fancy, Mr Lockwood. You could not open a book in this library that I have not looked into, and got something out of also – unless it be that range of Greek and Latin, and that of French; and those I know one from the other. It is as much as you can expect of a poor man's daughter. However, if I am to follow my story in true gossip's fashion, I had better go on.

Has Lockwood doctored the story? Is Nelly Dean tailoring it to suit the person she's telling it to? Housekeeper to master (with a necessary degree of deference)? Homebody to young, naïve comer in bed with a chill seeking to alleviate boredom?

Is her phrase "in true gossip's fashion" a mite satirical? It is quite conceivable that the whole thing is a leg-pull. V.S. Pritchett has this to say of her:

> There is a faint, homely pretence that Nelly, the housekeeper and narrator, is a kindly, garrulous old body; but look at her. It is not concealed that she is a spy, a go-between, a secret opener of letters. She is a wonderful character, as clear and round as any old nurse in Richardson or Scott; but no conventional sentiment encases her. She is as hard as iron and takes up her station automatically in the battle.[1]

Nelly is not the independent observer we would like her to be. She has been a participant in the events she describes, sometimes affecting the course they run; she has opinions and partialities; for all her commonsense, she admits to superstition. In the words of F.H. Langman:

> Nelly is not merely a witness. She is a creature of will, and she exerts this will to some effect. Her narrative is deeply coloured not only by her 'conventional values' but also by her private motives: her personal loyalties and her need to protect herself. This is true of others as well. There is a constant suggestion of bias in the narration, leading at times to incompatible versions of what happened. All the narration involves recollection, selection, and emphasis; and the author shows a keen awareness of how the personality of the speaker may rearrange and even falsify what actually occurred.[2]

In this sense *Wuthering Heights* anticipates films like Kurosawa's *Rashomon* and Lawrence Durrell's sequence of novels *The Alexandria Quartet* where multiple versions of the same story are offered us. It means our view of the characters in *Wuthering Heights* and the judgements of them we are trying to formulate cannot help but be much more intricately complex and consequently not much better than provisional. In the end – and this is quite miraculous

– we are persuaded to the view that the characters have independent existences outside us and outside the novel. Like Hamlet, Emily Brontë's characters refuse to be pinned down. Remember, earlier we suggested that *Wuthering Heights* was a book a ghost was trying to get into and a haunted man trying to get out of. What it achieves, paradoxically, is an extraordinary realism.

Lockwood, presumably an educated man of his time, relies on reason to interpret the world and in large measure to protect himself from it. Emily Brontë destroys this illusion in the first three chapters. Nelly's common sense ("steady, reasonable kind of body") is illusory too: ultimately it cannot cope with the experiences she describes; it has limitations. At the end of the novel, even the loyal Joseph, we are surprised to discover, is glad to be released from Heathcliff, giving "thanks that the lawful master [Hareton Earnshaw] and the ancient stock were restored to their rights"; and we learn "the country folks, if you ask them, would swear on the Bible that he *walks*". The little lad and the sheep know this too. Nelly's common sense turns out to be fallible, untrustworthy: she tries to dismiss these sightings but admits: "I don't like being out in the dark now, and I don't like being left by myself in this grim house." Lockwood complacently walks away from the graves. Nelly goes on with her sewing. What has happened is literally beyond them.

Notes

[1] V.S. Pritchett, 'The Implacable, Belligerent People of Wuthering Heights', *New Statesman and Nation*, 22nd June 1946. Also printed in *Wuthering Heights: An Anthology of Criticism,* compiled by Alastair Everitt (Frank Cass & Co. Ltd, 1967).

[2] F.H. Langman 'Thoughts on *Wuthering Heights*', *Essays in Criticism*, XV, (July 1965). Also printed in *Wuthering Heights: An Anthology of Criticism*.

5

A Capital Fellow

Wuthering Heights is for the most part meticulously detailed, rooted in the specific, but there are elements in it that remain mysterious. We never know the reason for old Mr Earnshaw's sixty-miles-each-way walk to Liverpool and back or why – unless we infer it's simply philanthropic of him – he brings back the seven-year-old waif he finds on the streets there. This waif is dark-skinned, gypsy-like in appearance, and this has inevitably led commentators to speculate as to his origins. There are Brontë family stories that may have a bearing on the matter[1] but in the end it is part of the necessary effect Emily Brontë is carefully scoring for his background to remain obscure, whether he be Irish, gypsy, Lascar, illegitimate son, or whatever. The same can be said for Heathcliff's three-year absence and subsequent return. We know why he leaves so abruptly in August 1780, aged 16, but where he goes and what enables him to come back looking "tall, athletic, a well-formed man", with black whiskers half-covering his cheeks and with a pile of money in his pocket, is never made clear. In chapter 4 Nelly tells Lockwood: "He has nobody knows what money, and every year it increases", and later suggests that time spent in the army may account for it, but there's no evidence for this beyond his "upright carriage".

So Heathcliff – much as I would like to claim him as a fellow Scouser – is without origins (he may not have been born in Liverpool but brought there). He is also without name[2] until given the singular one that serves as both Christian name and surname ... though the word "Christian" here is somewhat incongruous. This single name gives him the sense of something elemental, archetypal. Significantly, it is the Christian name of an Earnshaw who had died in childhood. This means he is symbolically a brother to Hindley and Catherine. Given that Catherine and he grow up together as virtual brother and sister, this gives a distinctly uneasy air of incest to the novel, something which provides it with a link to the great tragedies of Oedipus and Lear (Lear's favouring his youngest daughter has that kind of edge to it; there is a reference to Lear at the end of chapter 2, albeit comic). In other words, with this Emily Brontë braves entry into taboo territory to the point of necrophilia. Where it doesn't go is sex. The relationship between Heathcliff and Catherine is, as pointed out earlier, an asexual one which can only find its consummation in death. One way of interpreting this may be to see it as a form of sublimation – passion made safe through idealisation. It is of great significance that Catherine's ghost is a pre-pubescent twelve and not the nineteen-year-old she died as. She remains a child, unaffected by sexual feelings. Joyce Carol Oates sees the novel as "a parable of innocence and loss, and childhood's necessary defeat" and describes it as "erected upon not only the accumulated tensions and part-formed characters of adolescent fantasy ... but upon the very theme of adolescent, even childish, or infantile, fantasy"; she goes on, later in her essay, to say: "Why the presumably robust Catherine Earnshaw's life should end, in a sense, at the age of twelve; why, as a married woman of nineteen, she should know herself irrevocably "changed" – the novel does not presume to explain. This is the substance of tragedy, the hell of tumult that is character and fate combined. Her passion for Heathcliff notwithstanding, Catherine's identification is with the frozen and peopleless void of an irrecoverable past and not with anything human."[3] There is something to be said for this assessment. One could argue, given that the death of Catherine and the birth of her daughter are virtually one and the same act, plus the fact that they own the same name, she is resurrected in her daughter who, by proxy, provides her with another chance to grow into a properly loving womanhood.

It goes without saying that the Liverpool waif, given the name Heathcliff, is deprived of parents, a virtual orphan, and it is worth pointing out that this is part of a pattern we find in the novel: children deprived of parents. The old Earnshaws die – Mrs Earnshaw in 1773 when Catherine is eight and Hindley sixteen; her husband, leaving his favourite, Heathcliff, exposed, dies in 1777. The second Catherine loses her mother almost immediately after her birth, and her father when she is seventeen; Mr And Mrs Linton die in 1780 as a direct consequence of Catherine Earnshaw's fever in 1780, when Edgar is eighteen and Isabella fifteen; Linton Heathcliff is deprived of a father by being removed to London by his mother, who dies in 1797 when he is thirteen; Hareton loses his mother (Frances) just a few months after his birth, and his father (Hindley) when he is six years old.[4] They are all consequently made vulnerable to ill-treatment.

Heathcliff is also part of another thematic pattern already alluded to, which starts with Lockwood – that of the resented intruder. He has been called "the intrusive bringer of doom";[5] he is no consolation for the lost whip and mangled fiddle old Earnshaw promised to bring back from Liverpool for Catherine and Hindley. Heathcliff is the cuckoo in the nest: Hindley hates him, and so in the beginning does Nelly. Even Catherine "showed her humour by grinning and spitting at the stupid little thing". The passion that eventually develops and holds him and Catherine together as soul-mates is "offset by ... Hindley's resentment against the intruder, a resentment that is given full play after Mr Earnshaw's death".[6]

Heathcliff is someone we necessarily feel ambivalent about: we know of (or more accurately are told about) and condemn his brutal behaviour in the novel, but are also given mitigations for it. Is he as bad as the image of him that we have been presented with by the book's narrators? Hindley's behaviour is without doubt the worst in the book: Hindley has no saving graces, and the vengeance exacted on him by Heathcliff has at least a poetic justice to it. Heathcliff may be intolerant of weakness, but in some instances the reader is asked to see weakness as despicable and as perhaps deservedly attracting the treatment given to it. On occasion we are asked to take a more sympathetic of him than we may feel able to, as if the image we are forming of him (like Isabella's view of him as a devilish monster) is at risk of being a distortion. Nelly tells Isabella: "'Hush, hush! He's a human being,' I said. 'Be more charitable. There are worse men than he is yet.'" This kind of intrusion is unsettling to the reader: how do we tell the truth from what is in effect a version or versions of it? Can we ever really know what makes people tick? The effect is, as Langman insists, to "make the reader vaguely mistrustful, cautious in passing judgement", going on to say of Heathcliff that judgement of him "is inhibited, to a degree, by the thought that the case against him has been exaggerated by the bias of the narrators".[7]

Notes

[1] See the website:
http://www.wuthering-heights.co.uk/inspirations.htm

[2] There is, however, a curious irony in that Catherine Earnshaw/ Linton ends up anonymous – as simply "a woman" in the report of the shepherd boy. And before he was adopted by old Earnshaw Heathcliff was originally anonymous.

[3] *The Magnanimity of Wuthering Heights* by Joyce Carol Oates. See website http://www.usfca.edu/-southerr/wuthering.html

[4] *Wuthering Heights*, as previously stated, is filled with premature deaths. They are famously present in Charlotte's *Jane Eyre* too. John Lucas has reminded me that the 1840s were a bad time for family deaths from cholera epidemics. "It was these that finally persuaded government to give cities their charters so they could begin their own sanitation works, build pumping stations etc."

[5] Harry Blamires, *A Short History of English Literature* (Methuen, 1974).
[6] Ibid.
[7] Ibid.

6

In April Then

There are readers – probably in the majority – for whom the novel is above all 'about' the love between Heathcliff and the first Catherine, because of the way it touches on hidden feelings and profound yearnings and even, as I've suggested, taboo subjects – readers who, like Keats, long "for a Life of sensations rather than of Thoughts".[1] In addition to this, Heathcliff radiates an obvious powerful sexual energy that some find irresistible. As a consequence, the second generation's story is often regarded as less effective, less absorbing. Pritchett for example rightly calls the novel "a book which *feels* human beings, as they feel themselves ..." but he goes on to admit: "I am one of those who are not carried on by the second part of the story. I can see its moral necessity, but I do not *feel* its logic ... the high power has gone, the storm has spent its force ... only when [Heathcliff] begins to relive that ineluctable love, does the power return."[2]

Yet it is possible, as we have seen with Joyce Carol Oates, to regard the relationship as a projection of adolescent fantasy intolerant of the world as it is and twisted out of shape by fatal choices and ill-treatment. It is not just a matter of chance but of decision and will too – even if it seems to be without benefit of conscience. I say 'seems' because at the end of chapter 33 both Nelly and Joseph attribute the terminal decline of Heathcliff to conscience:

> He began to pace the room, muttering terrible things to himself, till I was inclined to believe, as he said Joseph did, that conscience had turned his heart to an earthly hell.

There is irony in this: we have been made to believe he had been living in an earthly hell of separation from the very time of Catherine's death.

Heathcliff and Catherine are victims of their own choices as well as of circumstances. She betrays her true nature, divides herself against herself, by making a wrong choice in marrying Edgar, with consequences that are literally fatal; Heathcliff's vengeance against Hindley can be explained but not talked away; the determination to acquire both the properties of Wuthering Heights and Thrushcross Grange, ruining two families in the process, may be viewed as the product of a kind of monomania hard to feel at ease with. We have seen that it can be argued that neither Catherine nor Heathcliff is suited to grown-up life. They are rebellious, passionate characters who can only truly exist together independent of compromise and the life of society (and exist *outside* the novel) – initially at a pre-pubescent level. And yet, the desire to be at-one with the universe, to merge with an elemental otherness, to shun attachment and escape time and the processes of change, to trade becoming for being, is at the heart of religious experience, deeply rooted in our natures, and sometimes brought sharply to the surface in all of us through sudden loss and separation. It is important to register the fact that Heathcliff's death represents a release as well as a consummation for both of them: it releases his beloved Catherine from her limbo of wandering solitariness and of being a child-ghost. What the shepherd boy reports having seen is "Heathcliff and *a woman* yonder, under t' nab" (my italics).

On the whole most people prefer or are happy to settle for love of a different kind – for content and mutual respect. It is this kind that is on offer in the coming together of the second Catherine and Hareton. It may be considered redemptive too, the calm after the storm, peace of mind once all passion's spent, new beginnings. If Catherine Earnshaw's marriage to Edgar was short-sightedly "wrong", her daughter's to Hareton (now that the Heathcliffian virus is out of her system), has every chance of being right. Cathy has learnt patience, compassion, humility: she is capable of sharing herself with others. She understands what Blake meant in 'Proverbs of Hell' when he wrote: "The most sublime act is to set another before you", and the kind of selfless love celebrated in his poem 'The Clod and the Pebble' where the humble Clod tells us:

> Love seeketh not itself to please,
> Nor for itself hath any care,
> But for another gives its ease,
> And builds a Heaven in Hell's despair.

It is often pointed out that the second part of the story – in which Heathcliff is mostly kept in the wings and only brought back in once he is dead – is more lyrical in nature. It is springtime, sunshine and flowers. Of the second Catherine, Nelly says: "I fancy no one could see Catherine Linton and not love her" – which has a certain irony to it in that Lockwood, to whom this is being said (does Nelly suspect this?), has from his first sight of her felt something of this. The love she offers and inspires is not a destructive, consuming passion, like that of Blake's 'Pebble':

> Love seeketh only Self to please,
> To bind another to its delight,
> Joys in another's loss of ease,
> And builds a Hell in heaven's despite.

It is made of gentleness and mildness, less passion than compassion, a force for health and goodness, like the force, in Dylan Thomas's poem, "that through the green fuse drives the flower". She loves her father dearly and tries her best to love Linton; it is her love that helps disarm Heathcliff and gives her the courage to stand up to him; it helps

Hareton, through careful nurturing, to grow straight, until "both their minds tending to the same point – one loving and desiring to esteem, and the other loving and desiring to be esteemed – they contrived in the end to reach it".

But Cathy is no simple goody-goody: she has inherited some of her mother's characteristics and features (people remember her eyes – eyes that are a source of torment to Heathcliff): she has her vitality, some of her independent spirit, which sometimes makes her disobedient. She is quite capable of tormenting Hareton by laughing at his clumsiness, his lack of social know-how, and his ignorance. At one point she hits him with a whip as he is trying to apologise for exposing his jealousy of Linton.

She suffers cruelly – she has been kidnapped, kept from her dying father, forced into marriage, and given more than one savage beating by Heathcliff. Zillah's view in chapter 30 is "the more hurt she gets, the more venomous she grows" – a familiar pattern in the novel. Zillah also tells us: "she has no lover or liker among us; and she does not deserve one". All of which might serve to support the view offered earlier that Nelly is as much an unreliable narrator as Lockwood: she dotes on Cathy and this colours her account.

But I think we can reasonably say that Cathy is a survivor – in this life, not the next. Love in her, despite being suppressed and thwarted, does not die. It is the death of others that frees her to blossom again. The dramatic change registered in Lockwood's final visit to Wuthering Heights in September 1802 has the quality of happy surprise. It is a lovely autumnal day: there are flowers, significantly imported from Thrushcross Grange (the two houses are now joined in a different way). We find Cathy patiently teaching Hareton; they are so respectably and elegantly dressed that Lockwood hardly recognises them; Nelly is in the kitchen "sewing and singing a song".

In the second part of the book (though 'second' is too simplistic a word) it is hard to like Heathcliff (but are we ever meant to like or dislike him?). He says things like "It's odd what a savage feeling I have to anything that is afraid of me"; he treats his own son barbarously; Cathy is treated no better; and he tries to mould (or is it distort?) Hareton's character to his liking. (It is important to note that Hareton retains real affection for him to the end.) His obsessive greed to possess both houses is usually seen as a betrayal of his true nature. But, as the novel insists, he is a man locked in the suffering of separation, tortured for 18 years' isolation from the one thing that gives his existence meaning. Eighteen years in which to endure "a strange way of killing, not by inches, but by fractions of hair-breaths". This agony helps to explain (but not necessarily excuse) his behaviour; he has been a haunted man for all this time, has lived with a ghost, and waited for the moment that ghost will bring him final release. His total absorption in his agony causes him to see reminders of his Catherine everywhere he looks: he sees her face in flagstones, in the face of her daughter: "the entire world is a dreadful collection of memoranda that she did exist, and that I have lost her". But then he mysteriously loses "the faculty of their destruction", becomes more determinedly solitary, stops eating: the ghost has "communicated apparently pleasure and pain in exquisite extremes"; and when it comes, his death is medically unfathomable; his eyes won't close and his face wears a sneer. Hareton kisses what is described as his "sarcastic, savage face". The lattice window is banging, as it did for Lockwood, and his body is soaked with rain. We are told the window "had grazed one hand that rested on the sill". In this way the novel comes full circle. Can we say Heathcliff has lived out his punishment and earned the consummation devoutly to be wished of reunion with his soul-mate? Are we happy for him? Or are we content to say goodbye to him and release him to the elements and so look forward to New Year's Day, 1803? Why the sarcastic look on his face? Is it for all those weaklings left behind? Why not a look of ecstasy, of attainment?

The novel also comes full circle in the prospect of marriage of Cathy and Hareton, where the mingling of genes (in contrast to the mingling of dusts in the grave) is wholly positive, as if it cures all the sickliness that has cursed both families. The motif of orphaned children finds a resolution through Nelly, who tells Lockwood that Cathy and Hareton are now "in a measure [her] children".[3]

One is tempted to consider the loves of Heathcliff and Catherine and of her daughter and Hareton, like the two houses, as representing two sides of our natures: the if-only and the yes-but of dream and reality, of idealism and common sense, animus and anima, ying and yang; as well as aspects of nature: storm and calm, winter and spring, moorland and cultivated fields, misanthropist's Heaven and the stir of society. But again this sounds simplistically dualistic: the natures of the characters in the novel are mixed. We know this from the start with Lockwood, whose good manners belie a cruelty. And what did Catherine and Heathcliff see when they looked through the windows of the "posh" Thrushcross Grange but two spoilt children pettishly arguing and abusing a puppy? Thrushcross Grange is private property, and, though the home of an upholder of the law (Linton is a magistrate), is guarded by dogs and burly servants. Old Linton is outraged by the intrusion: "To beard a magistrate in his stronghold, and on a Sabbath, too!" he exclaims. Class distinction maintained by force.[4]

Notes

[1] Letter to Benjamin Bailey, 22nd November 1817.

[2] Ibid.

[3] See Juliet Barker's comprehensive biography, *The Brontes* (Weidenfeld and Nicolson, 1995). There she makes the point that the relationship between "Linton and Catherine, in particular, is essentially that of a mother surrogate and her child".

[4] "It is worth noting that throughout the 19th century class plays off against love to break relationships and produce a definite form of 19th century tragedy, all the way from *Wuthering Heights* to – say – *The Woodlanders* and via *Great Expectations* and, in poetry Tennyson's *Maud* ... *Wuthering Heights* is probably the first great work to take up this subject, though there are hints in earlier work ... *Emma*, and, more teasingly, *Barnaby Rudge,* set at more or less the same time as *Wuthering Heights*." John Lucas.

Endpiece

The kind of experience Emily Brontë is trying to describe in *Wuthering Heights* is not altogether containable in words. The nearest she can get to it is paradox ("Nelly, *I am* Heathcliff! ... he's more myself than I am") and dream, in which the laws of time and place do not apply and which she contrives to make us believe, are more real than real. Dorothy Van Ghent attempts to describe the experience in terms of the "dark Otherness, by which the soul is related psychologically to the inhuman world of pure energy".[1] Whatever consummation Heathcliff and Catherine may be said to achieve it is not one that is possible in life and it is life they leave behind for the rest of us to get on with: Lockwood blithely walks away from the grave, Nelly has her maternal care of Cathy and Hareton to enjoy. The marriage of these two happens without us. It is, as we said earlier, readers who linger a little while longer than Lockwood, gazing at the three headstones in Gimmerton churchyard and wondering what kind of story we have been profoundly imaginatively immersed in and how much of it we can really believe, before we too eventually move off, still a bit dazed, to get on with the business of living.

Notes

[1] Dorothy Van Ghent, *The English Novel: Form and Function* (Harper and Row, 1968).

GREENWICH EXCHANGE BOOKS

STUDENT GUIDE LITERARY SERIES

The Greenwich Exchange Student Guide Literary Series is a collection of essays on major or contemporary serious writers in English and selected European languages. The series is for the student, the teacher and 'common readers' and is an ideal resource for libraries. The *Times Educational Supplement* praised these books, saying, "The style of [this series] has a pressure of meaning behind it. Readers should learn from that ... If art is about selection, perception and taste, then this is it."

(ISBN prefix 978-1-871551 applies unless marked*****, when the prefix 978-1-906075 applies.)

The series includes:
Antonin Artaud by Lee Jamieson (98-3)
W.H. Auden by Stephen Wade (36-5)
Honoré de Balzac by Wendy Mercer (48-8)
William Blake by Peter Davies (27-3)
The Brontës by Peter Davies (24-2)
Robert Browning by John Lucas (59-4)
Lord Byron by Andrew Keanie (83-9)
Samuel Taylor Coleridge by Andrew Keanie (64-8)
Joseph Conrad by Martin Seymour-Smith (18-1)
William Cowper by Michael Thorn (25-9)
Charles Dickens by Robert Giddings (26-9)
Emily Dickinson by Marnie Pomeroy (68-6)
John Donne by Sean Haldane (23-5)
Ford Madox Ford by Anthony Fowles (63-1)
The Stagecraft of Brian Friel by David Grant (74-7)
Robert Frost by Warren Hope (70-9)
Patrick Hamilton by John Harding (99-0)
Thomas Hardy by Sean Haldane (33-4)
Seamus Heaney by Warren Hope (37-2)
Joseph Heller by Anthony Fowles (84-6)
Gerard Manley Hopkins by Sean Sheehan (77-3)
James Joyce by Michael Murphy (73-0)
Philip Larkin by Warren Hope (35-8)
Laughter in the Dark – The Plays of Joe Orton by Arthur Burke (56-3)
George Orwell by Warren Hope (42-6)
Sylvia Plath by Marnie Pomeroy (88-4)

Poets of the First World War by John Greening (79-2)
Philip Roth by Paul McDonald (72-3)
Shakespeare's *A Midsummer Night's Dream* by Matt Simpson (90-7)
Shakespeare's *King Lear* by Peter Davies (95-2)
Shakespeare's *Macbeth* by Matt Simpson (69-3)
Shakespeare's *The Merchant of Venice* by Alan Ablewhite (96-9)
Shakespeare's *Much Ado About Nothing* by Matt Simpson (01-9)*
Shakespeare's Non-Dramatic Poetry by Martin Seymour-Smith (22-6)
Shakespeare's *Othello* by Matt Simpson (71-6)
Shakespeare's Second Tetralogy: *Richard II–Henry V* by John Lucas (97-6)
Shakespeare's Sonnets by Martin Seymour-Smith (38-9)
Shakespeare's *The Tempest* by Matt Simpson (75-4)
Shakespeare's *Twelfth Night* by Matt Simpson (86-0)
Shakespeare's *The Winter's Tale* by John Lucas (80-3)
Tobias Smollett by Robert Giddings (21-1)
Alfred, Lord Tennyson by Michael Thorn (20-4)
Dylan Thomas by Peter Davies (78-5)
William Wordsworth by Andrew Keanie (57-0)
W.B. Yeats by John Greening (34-1)

FOCUS Series
Emily Brontë's ***Wuthering Heights*** by Matt Simpson (10-1)*
T.S. Eliot's ***The Waste Land*** by Matt Simpson (09-5)*
Thomas Hardy: ***Poems of 1912–13*** by John Greening (04-0)*
The Poetry of Ted Hughes by John Greening (05-7)*

Other subjects covered by Greenwich Exchange books
Biography
Education
Philosophy